Collateral Light

poems by

Julia Cohen

Brooklyn Arts Press · New York

ISBN-13: 978-1-936767-22-9

Cover art by Simone Shubuck. Overall design by Joe Pan.

Published in The United States of America by:
Brooklyn Arts Press
154 N 9th St #1
Brooklyn, NY 11249
www.BrooklynArtsPress.com
info@brooklynartspress.com

Distributed to the trade by Small Press Distribution / SPD
www.spdbooks.org

Library of Congress Cataloging-in-Publication Data

Cohen, Julia.
[Poems. Selections]
Collateral Light / by Julia Cohen.
    pages ; cm
ISBN 978-1-936767-22-9 (pbk. : alk. paper)
I. Title.

PS3603.O366C65 2013
811'.6--dc23
                        2013004200

10 9 8 7 6 5 4 3 2 1

First Edition

My thanks to the editors who have included the following poems in their journals:

1913	"Not the Fact of the Burning Forest but the Scent of the Burning"
Colorado Review	"Collateral Light"
Dusie	"Call Me a Grown-Up but My Five Eyes Blink at Once"
Esque	"Is It Hard to Count the Times I Am Deliberate?"
	"The Place We Worry About"
Everyday Genius	"Bird, Bring Me That Finger"
Ghost Town	"Someday You Will Be So Long"
	"Sad Paint"
	"Invention of the Outside World"
Harp & Altar	"I Carry a Basket for the Fingers That Fall"
Hawai'i Review	"Romantic Weather"
jubilat	"We Clamor We Like the Sound of It"
Lamination Colony	"You've Handed Me Something That Will Never Dry"
New American Writing	"No One Told Me I Was the Arrow"
	"The Room Deformed the Sound of It"
Notnostrums	"Fill Me with Poison!"
	"I Have a White Napkin Strapped to My Head"
Octopus	"For the H in Ghost"
OH NO	"We're Enamored with Shadows"
	"They Hover They Do Whatever"
Sixth Finch	"The Decoy Museum Is Still"
So & So	"A Bright Wire Flown"
	"What Was Record"
Spoke Too Soon	"Practice by Fire & Doubt"

CONTENTS

Collateral Light

THE INCLUSION OF OBJECTS

You are

my sticky, flammable

folder, child, alive

I.

My face was curious

NO ONE TOLD ME I WAS THE ARROW

I'm chalky
from
banged up
stars

To face the sand
is a false start

Spruces
& their red coats
eye-pop the mountain
like a dog's wounded
side

A car will take
you away

Embryonic dish soap
& the also-sky

**

I caught
a life
of sea-
sickness
dreaming of ships

An insect
on snow

At the limit
of our
body
a brief spasm
of laurels

Jostle me
into a winter-
wave

Damp & cylindrical

I raised
a black rooster
tipping
the color
of my red
heart's name

I sharpen
my point

plunge
into a glass
of soil

SOMEDAY YOU WILL BE SO LONG

I put the wrong name on
so my ribs push in & a sound
appears like oOO0o0O0ooo
like falling off the tire swing

Someday you'll be so long
Your body stretches it doesn't
know how it got here

Tunnel running?
By the fur?

Blood in the meadow—to spill well
The black flowers like pinwheels
spin & rotate heat in their starry fists

Volatile alkali in your absence
I sleep next to the phone
Its whole body fits
on the pillow

The value of
this process lies
in the possibility
of checking

A name fitted to
your whooshing sound

Sleepers decrease
the classic movement
of a running dog

I have counted out
all the apples you will

ever eat & all the arms
to possibly swing you

Then the cliff
no one saw coming

Ground down
I sling pillows
over the spills

FILL ME WITH POISON!

Over there they call words
the children
of dead people

or crisp folds in
the hushing linens

they call out *finish, children*

**

maybe you're movement—
the kind that can look
back, stick an index
finger in an atom

nobility is not a feeling
cunning is not a feeling
decency is not a feeling

A feeling not an empty space

Here a localized wanting, a text
among animals & aprons

The raccoon makeup you'll wipe
off to reconcile?

**

Disassemble the atom
& behold the infinite subject!

Sense-data poised for
takeoff

For the red handed
the red-handed face

Here in a willful habitat
the cult of affirmation & joy

What's your capacity for mutation?
Don't remove yourself
from the experiment

We dress the atom in
pajamas with feet

**

Too much
Too much of what?

The no not yet quiet nor
the yeses stinging their way
out of your toothpaste tube

The dark-aired, overturned canoe
brimming with human

as the word ranunculus roughs up
its own petals

A BRIGHT WIRE FLOWN

I stemmed the verge
of your night-garden

Whatever's real dies
& mitigates the quantity

I unhooked the flower

Up up up   up
There you go

INVENTION OF THE OUTSIDE WORLD

My face was curious
I looked up
the scientific purpose of revenge

Then the daffodilic
gave way to an uncertain moon
frost-pinched & antsy

Clouds as thought bubbles
Winter fall-out

Revenge stems from those who tire
of holding up
this enormous apple
Its fontanel the thumb-bruise

Twin wings
scuttling between a smoked limb
& the refrigerator house

Conch shell dentata, the doctor
of your heart-beat

I have a cabbage-head?
I am spewing blood?
You vultures, at this point you
should know better

Culture is the option to
choose not to die

An atonal umbrella or
ivory dominoes
stored in a lunchbox
when it pours

IS IT HARD TO COUNT THE TIMES
I AM DELIBERATE?

I am visceral!
Just like you
The interplay

Just like paintings
The feelings

I crouch down
& spring up whenever
whenever anyone enters

There are plants you can
hug or hide behind

Mimicry should be deliberate
Love should be deliberate
& generous

Nothing peripheral
to the implied

We gaze at the mother-vine

What part of ourselves
are we sparing?

No! Love should not
deliberate
or you'll write the word wine
with ink
to attain permanent
wine

There is a foxtrot
in your march

THE ROOM DEFORMED THE SOUND OF IT

I took the whir
out of the hamper

Everything I do
is very grainy

My pixels
deflect arrows

Gradual welts immerge
complimentary effects of
ribs & leaves

**

I learn to digest
I learn organism
I zipped the moth
into the knapsack

At night babies are
delivered

Shake the immense
reciprocal
The breathing landscape
let's not forget about that

Here shadows have legs
The trees the trees make
no mistakes

**

I battered a dead moth
by riding home

I travel over
a planet like this
& increments crumble

I hear weather
Nothing but wind
in fur, little cliff
of a jar
I tilt to you

Our hands are
the Woolslayer

We bundle particles
We irradiate paper
We share a feather

**

A moment mistaken
for the pixeled wing

I unzip your leafmouth
to ask do babies
still fall from trees?

Distortion lengthening
the arrow

BIRD, BRING ME THAT FINGER

with the tied twine
a syllable of labor

The outstretched match
red-capped & wooden
O oxygen-clutching

But I gather light nor
heat nor claw will keep

Dress of intricate patterns:
blue candy wrappers, pollen
an invitation viewed through a veil

But if I keep asking you or throw
a cute command what
lock is cut?

The last pages of pity, feed them
to the web
naked & washing dishes

Drag the white bone
as a souvenir of fire

THE PLACE WE WORRY ABOUT

To work away from utility
I profiled through a paper fence

Blue lines, yellow paper

Color has me
I imagine

**

A formation of water wheels
A formation of organs

Movement caught in the work

A house is easily checked

To pass by & ask "Will I remember
this?" then later to remember only
the question?

**

Plastic analysis

of a house rhythmically
in gardens

To shuck the silken

**

An accent misplaced
Slackness of violets
In opposition to the place we worry

As evidence effects the afternoon

How real the object
remains despite all abstractions
A violet rash

THEY HOVER THEY DO WHATEVER

Sliding water, will it reappear
as the dim
pause of distress?

Remains are
for those in animal masks

Do you give to avoid?
The gust caught
an impatient arrow

The dead shepherd
an improvisation
to distrust

I went home
a guest
from the funeral
with the present generation

COLLATERAL LIGHT

I put my face
inside your face

& look down
at the sunken garden

My toes are cute

My packet of
bees comes in

**

Pour your wicked
cornstalks over my what

Everyone likes to look
at the moon

Show me mine

Chew a page

Here comes something

**

Play with
the biggest face

Do you get a bee?

Blue is a very
good color

You happen

Here

I am watching bees
traverse your jeans

I bit the point
of the strawberry

Off to the left
I'm seeding

The light peels back
a ringing splint

**

I can photograph
what scares me?

I'm a clotted drainpipe

Get a ladder
Guts

Any sky is the best sky

Trees scratch out

**

Catch a stick
a log
a house to comb

Last leaf

I decided on time

Yet teeth

II.

I can't just sit here with feelings

SOMEDAY YOU'LL BE REPLACED BY
LANGUAGE & THEN NOTHING AT ALL

I killed the beast & then I became the beast
      Whatever I ask for turns red
watery

I climbed the stairs before the staircase
      I'm to blame
Your first image bounced back   the real ear
sits in the chest

No decision   in when my blood flows

**

The fruit fuzzed over   browned
as the marrow
      your teeth grind
out of the flattened bone   sidewinding

Knock the notch from the tree & tack it
      to my back like a doorknob
Don't you want your fingers

      to puppet my organs?

No? You'll learn one thing no one else
in this world knows

**

I can't just sit here with feelings   I wear
      the frame of the glasses without glass
so you touch my eyes

It's not cloud-anger it's that I see what can't
hold me

A musical introduction or vapors   lifting a
sovereign's home

**

Land documented our word-beheadings
          I could live inside a wave
if you gave me a chance   if I neared the water

Kiss my puppy lips my deer lips
the animal inside that animal
          alive & yelping through the skin

**

If nothing lived on then what's that
coughing?

You can't bury yourself inside   your child
Photogram of a wave & a doorknob falling
          to the floor

Though there's nothing more yellow than this melon

          You wouldn't think to need
a lucky number
to live on like the wristwatch   of a dead soldier

What I cut I open   to revision

NOT THE FACT OF A BURNING FOREST
BUT THE SCENT OF THE BURNING

A clear bottle with white liquid or
a white bottle fat   with bloody paper & the voyeur

Something bad happens & I like
its scent   I said follow me to   the black pasture
Reveal how to crunch
grass which isn't frozen   so we can lasso whatever moves

      With our rubber-stamps   we can fertilize
what sleeps below us   so I stick
my hand down your jeans & kill
you   like justice's torn-out-jaw
Call anger the first political   emotion

**

Until he was four my brother spoke only one
word: rooster   until he reached the mailbox   turns to
his mother *But what mail would come for me?*

The white bottle wobbled in its frame like something
that could be your friend   to drain the luxury pond
      I strap my goodbye-eyes on   step back
step closer   step back   this is reckoning

**

Look over the shoulder of your mother
legroom   flyleaf   try to destabilize
the center but the center
glides below you   like an angry child
drifting under a frozen pond

The smooth spleen moves   when you move

**

But I want to give you a new feeling   one you can't
get rid of right away
but in the end   it's just a white bottle
        I don't believe that either

My wooden knife I carve with the metal knife
It's hard to tuck yourself into bed so that the blanket
        folds above your shoulders

CALL ME A GROWN-UP BUT
MY FIVE EYES BLINK AT ONCE

When I dug in the backyard I knew nothing   could cut me
Soft hair & a mind   trenching memory like dirt
like how the sound & taste of chewing snow is the same

My frequency framed in chives & locust-drawings
against fevered whiteness dipped   in fevered whiteness

**

Meet at the juniper where the creek turns east
For reckoning retain the ticket
366 days in a leap year   cognate child

A dedication in the microphone: fury of velveteen
that was 18 years ago
You only feel invincible twice in your life

To dissect the rarified heart
    especially bird

**

Primordial fronds with 3D daffodils in the dreamscape
    chase large rodents into the ghost forest:

the animal in my right arm was a superhero cape
    a cape to give the younger brother with a hammer
the animal in my leg was the deep humiliation
of crawling up the stairs

    If the fever is age or anxiety   can I lean in
& sweep the whiteness away

I miss the charm of a sturdy memory like a missing limb

**

Now I can't stop gripping   with my neck
if I have to

I can't reenact the conversations
though I won't coat myself with milk paint

I see bodies but the words are gone   They took place
near a lake eaten by fevered whiteness
        as if a stone sums up the land that stands behind it

In the distance   a soft child counting a sequence
of ants or misters

**

Spidery arrangements   a child unnamed for safety
to double back & throw myself off   my own trail

I'm only embarrassed when I embarrass   you
the deepest well I ever fell into

Too busy relaying information to absorb it
"I didn't write it I only wrote / it down"

a hammer eliminates the need for help?

Drift-wood finish   basis of the charm
signs of soft child activity   show up least
the marks of hammers

Fever takes you like an undertow   like mister

**

Help remember   calm me down to remember

I spelled my name with mud & sold it at a lemonade stand

If you misplace directions for making the deception
you want to make   use blood to color the milk paint
behind the fence   a curtsey

Anyone is anyone else because   deep down
they have a face?

Dab a little water without disease

**

It's exhausting   everyone asking to feel alive!

But I drew an incorrect candle or I drew the perfect
candle   & it was still rejected

The last 7 seconds watch the body roll away
from the head

That log is not a bridge when the mud dries

Somewhere I am a goldenchild
     where I speak for the poem

Now beat   back against what you made

I CARRY A BASKET FOR
THE FINGERS THAT FALL

The nests outside swing wider
than my house   my hilltop
the crest on the mantel calling   for veins

When I fork this light two bodies
        blend into the face you held
Jumbled letters   glisten on the backs
of flowers

In the frozen garden I feel
fetching   how I met you   how sleep
        mists our daily envies

so the ovals upturn & open

**

Small breaths penny   the floor
into soft nooks & wetness
        descend down the chimney

When I take my gloves off
the water is   wetter
        tastes like the day I learned

to run with a basket of sheets

**

Don't back away from
the face's missing fingers   I'll be at the altar
of your sleepcoat   an emaciated tree

with my offer of nametags
      & a broken dinner plate

I've never moved slower

No oily necklace   no bicycle seats offer
      to cut the sheet into smaller sections

**

I could saw the trees into a bed
      to angle your sleep
though you'd still be sleeping

      Yelps from the chimney
are the victors

THE DECOY MUSEUM IS STILL

The decoy museum is still a real museum
so distracting   you can die inside & not
          even know it

Your whatness   your childhood-bird looks
so young   snow like gunpowder

Cough syrup on the collar of a white shirt
          something to hide under the bed for

I reach back   into the body of your memory
& stick Post-it notes on the edge
          of every mirror

**

Cold grass on the floor & covered in sugar
the slurred satellite   of your swing set

I fashioned the raincoat   to keep rain

on your inside   an apple tree sprouts in the blue
          Oldsmobile's brown cushion

**

The decoy museum   lit by bayonets fresh
from the oven

cut with colleagues & the weaker version of lies

returns to the situation of a leaf
          brown paper & a misspent life

You walk into a stranger's dirty pocket of air

**

More than a replica   a lure
the birthdays range in anticipation   they fell for glory

Trouble distinguishing grids: a farm or a way
          to fire a person

Fake flowers burst forth from fake seeds
nothing ornamental   in the decoy museum

In a guild-like fashion   they lay it down
in a sound-like sound I take   it away

Those bandages   dirty pompoms need changing
          I let one emotion follow the other & believe
them both

**

Wing clipping season ends when I cut
the swans from your ankles   newspaper shin guards
are birthdays

Between the gilded   pages I whistle the grass
          between my thumbs
I destroy the like-like decoy   I've been meaning to
live

Place all possible coverings away from your face's reach
          what happens to your face?

I'VE WALKED BACKWARDS
TO REMEMBER MY NAME

Covered in lichen & night worms

Who touched my hands?
I've yet to find the warmest part   of my body

Not a name but the body   mud-tracked with hay
in the grips of thunder

apple-picking thunder   tar-thunder   sleeveless
thunder of soft child

If there is fear in my mind then fear in the poem then
the rose is a wolf   its nose keeps me cold

another assassin

**

The love I have   a demonstration of thunder

When I color your coloring book I won't
stay in the lines

an inside voice getting out

Not a name but the body greening   the telephone wire
bedlamp & semaphore

**

If you do not hear the voice   I have not
underspoken

Here is my body moving air out of the way
thunder in the inside voice

An arrangement of organs warms the forest
to flail to touch more

**

Knead the greening   my wrist a rolling pin
The warmest part of a name is the body
breaking away from its name
        a thunder-shook rose & molting colors

Turn your inside voice out
words flailing   then body-anchored

Flash me your white tail   of words
everything to offer

a soft child thing

FOR THE H IN GHOST

Taught to autograph the sandbox
who said our silky   signatures are indelible?
        In this erasure   to confess
we only possess ourselves

Stripped & succulent   as an anti-ode
to carelessness   posterity & Novocaine
Cut through the diagonal
        ocean for the antidote of amnesia

Simplicity of the greatest feat: hurt
as few as possible   Dry the heart's fog
Hold tight & how to let go

Valves open   close
The wet fullness of a Siberian pear

Even in shipwreck we are not
        marooned   We play host
to ghosts daily
Mother Father   the street sweeper

The unspeakable "H"
When the bar   falls away
"I" & "I" stand   face to face

I have antennae   I have a tail
I cloud-hop
        I know how to hold a hand

YOU'VE HANDED ME SOMETHING
THAT WILL NEVER DRY

I've lived in almost every room
but it's hard to match   the color
of your missing piece

The barn door is a table   I read over

My undercoat   a cluster of photographs
I kept from the fire

If I took the museum's view you would be wood-
cut & staring back

Scrape of a vintage empire   wax & cola
How do I explain hiding in the lumberyard
as cloth on your knuckles?

Your chemical form rises   in the photograph

I've just started mine   in tree-turrets
in radio germs stacked on cracked tires

Were you stained   for the same reason?

Here is the beauty of using wax
& you   finished of any age

My barn glows   not on fire   not of glass

III.

Open the invitation to anyone

THE MIND THIS MORNING

Play a little
lime-game with me

Your lake-face flashes
like a shelf
cleaned by the sweep
of an arm

Crash! Don't own
a broom
We collect
dust to collage
the dock

Someone watches
from behind a tree
like a water-clock

We exist before
sex
We float the rinds
in a bucket
I am a matchstick
mast

The source of joy
is the instinct for joy

When we play
the faster we spin
trees   mother   trees   mother
treesmothertrees

A MEMBER OF THE LIVING CLASS

I ate a cucumber covered in dirt
An owl caught in a triangle

Do you consider yourself vertical?
Over your face a magazine at dawn

**

Some say I'm hurling towards earth
earplugs blissed out on a pumpkin

Sleep snatched the war so what quickens?
Clang clang?

Raise your antennae arms
Your children busting

with adjectives, anti-statuaries
& a hanging bird

**

Are you reading in the street?
Between tires dice-teeth spark
like dolls aflame like a battle pulled back

Some say I'm close to docking in skirt or
shorts or a patch of paper

A handful of red-headed leaves
I'm bustling to show you

**

I admit my dog carries
a baby monkey on his back
A clan of clean socks the war casts off

Can you direct traffic?
Choose your fiancé?
Here are the replacement parts
tin pants

**

I'm islanding up

Some say I have little
faith in the full
sentence

Yet each hair
an arrow, a holograph
of teeth

A yurt for your sweetheart
Yogurt pailed & passed
around the wars

The bird submerged in a magazine

Some say they browsed
the first acorn

WHAT WAS RECORD

I miss bees in winter

Tuft, a treetop pushing
against the ceiling

Some say nothing
can mount the sky

A magnet under the ice
pulls the skater
toward me

I'm filled
with invisible arrows
& ice & ice

No buzz
Skinned to miss

A box is
human, a human
nest

The restness I compass
I forgive
the nuisance war?

Some say skin—
having done it

ROMANTIC WEATHER

Betrayal, an inverted orchid
clinging to a cloud

Wing & comb, who to the hymnal
anchored to eggshell?

A bell in the thicket, glowing

The taste almost condenses

O ominous sundial
I made the apple

I HAVE A WHITE NAPKIN
STRAPPED TO MY HEAD

For a while
each year I find
another one of my holes

Dark spots to explore
I have another
another

**

Old telephone calls
recording the parade
of babies bedizened & sinking bibs

**

Speaking in bubbles
welcome weightless holes

From the window to the roof
curved glass & cotton snubbed
An exit strategy for the night

I bury the dark behind
our house
in exigent avoidance

**

For a while
the record player turns off
on its own

I say *phew* when I click
the light switch

A curve of *this* shape?
Have another

THE RAISING

I know your mountain
It's flagless

Berry-laden, a face
of oily burlap
laced with roots

Ash on the envelope
To shake off or tuck in

Lakes, turn to me

Tumorless
I hold the water

YOU'LL SEE MY DESIGN INSIDE A LEMON

I thought of fish scales & drops
of war like a line of spiders

You leave marks in
the dirt & that's my pattern
Ants swarming a cut potato

They say joy
They say banish the foreign night
choked by childish branches

The wedding of war & a thatched roof
Take off your acorn hat

Children pop
out of boxes like lanterns released

Soldiers bury lemon buds
"Have you seen a muzzle on a bull?
What I use as my design?"

They say carve your potato to stamp
the envelope's white forearm

The pattern of a marriage
procession: hooves, hairpins, mud
meshed to scalp, motoring

They say children fall instantly
into use

Condense our lives inside
a single lemon

Seeds scatter on a feather
The weft you attach to foreheads

WE'RE ENAMOURED WITH SHADOWS

My hands unshakable apples
stripping your gallery

We're convinced arrows
have no shadows

Sick spoons
to sojourn & language

In stirrups, in banquette
unabashed

Open the invitation to anyone

The moon a bloody thumbprint
The one I left on your throat

What mood do you want?
Tonight?

YOUR HASTY ANSWER TO LIGHT

Horizon's vestige
a drama

Why does it slant pictorial?

Particular dark
a flighty bulb

I'm part-time liquid

Deficit of the pear
behind the ear

I made a motion, a motor
& a car cries back

Crossing out
the strain of light

Behind-behind
the liquid

SAD PAINT

A bird-covered tree—
what kind of person I am

Sirens crash through the pines
like a painting of a girl

kneeling in corners

hostage to hanging clouds
I hide my pills in

the clock I hear yet can't spot

My crust of bread points at you
like an index finger

to calendar the brush drying
against my cheek

of ants logging the insect home
of bangs balancing on eyelids

Three prongs of a shadow relent
the descent to wriggle loose

Okay so I don't want a sad
painting watching over us

IV.

Everything needs to be moved through

I STARED AT YOUR CAMERA
& PROMPTLY DIED

I cut myself   out of a colossal leaf
I dipped my head in the vein   of a calf
        Feathers poked out of my belly   like hands
that lead to the cloud-dynasty

Vaudeville laughed at my slouch-posture
but I snapped
        the raft it sat on & sank it
in the moat

But ice cubes melt in my pocket   they *melt*
        So how cruel could I be?

Without death no Classics manifest
        Instead of a flash   you sang the high note

Dip the dead owl in the slip & burn
its body to a shell   a mask   what comes to collect
you from the dripping shelf

        This darkness has no shade   chews the stalagmite down
to the wick   Oils & dirt from hands can
stain the formation   corduroy air

To wish I owned the method of delivery

All the trees covered in shells!   Sand dollars hanging
      from branches   Can I cross over your line?

Neck-sand   clean stone   What about the
other humanities? A red coat eaten by the tide lonely
like the discus

Climb out of the word-for-word crib

Are you   you aren't a patriot if you're closed to
the suggestion box   "purge   construct   stroke"
      That the plants are watered that the children tucked in—
that you dig under the fence to get here
Mountain of face

If I dug up all the lions by hand? If I stole the
shark's black purse of an egg?

My front yard chemical   Hold onto someone else
to stop twirling your hair

To love the patterns we didn't invent

Children in a circle shake & pass a jar of cream
        setting self-knowledge apart from self-interest
safely without   "us to destroy us"
        without butter glinting with glass

So coax that plasma out of bed!
Like your shadow sailing below you on your bike
        everything needs to be moved through

Tree pocked I trace loneliness in your sibling's land
        like history's never-resolved flings & assassins

Faked an aged era by turmeric   Tradition is a business
to escape from   to the warm body barn

Thicket of experience   you bracket in the yard
        Though when the leaves shrivel I see farther

Death is the opposite of dying slowly   balloon balloon

I doused myself in water & nothing   went out
        Is the window working?

I'm afraid it's all being acted out behind the garden sheets

The poem is the demand   Lean in like the steps
you made in woodshop

Cold water camp   Is nobody here?
        I can help you with those groceries

The lung-party   hosted by words
        hoisted into the branches
to dangle like a tire swing

If you hold the sheers I'll hold   the roots' hands
Shake out what's ripe to fall

        Watch it in my belly

If your first assessment of a lake is its perimeter
forego prayer for the face
Water slaps   laps up   eye-fauna

In which designated space would your trapped
door unfold?   If I do not spark?

Double-edged pen   a pile of piney breath
to defend or discard

Too hot for black dogs & the white dogs burn

Children desire dolls so they can name them   Desire
to name dolls as they are not   allowed to rename themselves

"I sleep jackknife tight" so grow up   handleless
        Reclaim words that have been taken
awe   rapture   grace   hunger

Dead-ringers for your unborn iris
        Horticulture eying the sidewalk for pamphlet-flutters

Poetry's death drive   the vaguer parts of speech

To mistake the glint of   your cell phone lid in the sun for
someone calling   August hail

During even the shower of spiders   I caught your
cuff I heard   *unlooked-for*   & looked into the fold

WE CLAMOR WE LIKE THE SOUND OF IT

C-major sky   what's your favorite shape of stammer?
O I have encountered you   quantum glitter
like my relationship to the river

I took
the word for fireworks
Found my mouth
in the knuckle rhyme
Let's visit the park we don't know

Arboretum of tenterhooks   we pour water in our dead
What are these crops of?
We keep snowballs in the freezer for the summer   to surprise it

It turns
out language
is the other people

Is another person's
language

Lunch alone at home   & I say to my face in the plate's glaze
This is the only life I have   I round up   Let's conspire

Are you sad?
Do you have wet hair?
The image is a mortal thing
To dwell, to leave traces

My lung a canoe caught   in the branches of a river   expands
like the night I learned to swim underwater   my lung contracts with fog
how I turn the light   off at daybreak

Ovarian cancer
Uterine cancer
Cervical cancer
Multiple sclerosis
Leukemia springing from the left leg

If my harvest isn't disease   guilt is a failure to hush when
our little pieces go pang   geranium & grapefruit
But if I'm caring for myself then who   am I not?
We clamor to reverberate

To bounce off of you claim
the tin-sound
Two pages stuck together

Packing disguised as unpacking
What if I need more time?
A wooden coin, your clogged nostril
Clods of grass we hold up like scalps

Has anyone noticed my arms are sparklers   The flaming kite cutting
the grass   I put my head inside the vase to hear the stems
If I've discarded my parts what makes this cave shape?

A sugar cube for each ant

Our plates pile up, chucked
out the window
Are your sounds *inside*
the paper asylum?

Glitter on the knuckle

Radishes & powdered mustard I place before you
red like by bleeding   I mean I blur I come together &   we're in
unison we're a parsnip party   we played out the language
A yellow tint your hair loosens

I caught you busting
a scab to wrench a scar
I cusped? We broke

the clasp of the orange
dress acquired through language
You didn't give me up or
you didn't give

I think about motion   about what I want to sustain
The sound of a fish tank   & now a bubble burst & now a world
There's nothing to scrape off the leaf-stained sidewalk

They jingled
They live on a bicycle farm

As all yellow is gold
they clamor & we let
them take that

V.

Let's worship doubt

PRACTICE BY FIRE & DOUBT

I.

Chanting novices like, where's my
tumultuous lock of hair?

A bonfire of troops drenched in pitch

I'm the girl with muscular wonder, fresh

with messengers of quivering medicine

Raised above the ground, the lonely
pile of distance binds in sleep

Girls in season? I ransack the animal?

Each hair moneyed to wheat or lentils

Bird's wings drop off & pelt the disease
personating limbs of a shrill tree

Faith coined to burn us out, survives the high
ranking field

Medicine-flames, the same species as hands

Let's worship doubt, let's make a day of it

Imbedded in cars, insects deliver
the birth of distant wars

II.

I'm shining my burnt broom with scandal
Habitual skin, habitual fuel

To brutish pity, disease tethers a vacant
throne & success of merchants

Down falls the casket like a white bird

I'm so buff
I'm a petite freak, a veil of

living green sprung from
the poetics of doubt

You see something, you feel
something, doubt

Tender veil of the buffering field
If you're the messenger then

the message swung from where?

Across the flames, midsummer sprouts
a dark branch, a cry that jumps

the threshold in your fatal color

Genital heat? Vegetal legs?

You throw out the dead
flowers to argue with a rosebud

III.

A body plunging into knowledge
A basket skims your table for

the faithful shoulder, a maneuver
like a barren mother

It's a particularly painful language

This, the process of majority

If you're waxy, then melt
If you like the sudden onset

of war, let me show you
the historical word for weather

Leather reigns & the plum's decay
Interference wafts like a disease

through your open window
Race like a natural death

The bird & I alternate inspecting
our mates, share dances

A girl lives in the form
of renewal, a rustic doubt

The hearth heated by a green
song, four hundred adoring words

chase the war into an idea, hair in your locket

Scales burn up, pitch forward like troops
budding across the branches of

a faithful summary

IV.

I'm cluttered with the touch
of coins & emptied by the touch of doubt

I'm bent on meeting the city
with two combustible hands

Is your clashing hungry? Can you
consolidate the animal?

Let's fatten the sacrificial thought

Are you the slanting face slicked with war?

I work out every other day
I call medicine my right hand man

Girls illustrate theories, girls sleepy
with distance, a girl the girl those girls

still devour
the throne back to this field

Acknowledgments

Thank you, entirely: Cynthia Arrieu-King, Sommer Browning, Robert J. Cataldo, Lisa Ciccarello, Arda Collins, Jennifer Denrow, Farrah Field, Brian Foley, Daniela Gesundheit, Heather Green, Jonathan Hamilton, Christopher Kondrich, Seth Landman, J. Michael Martinez, Keith Newton, Emily Pettit, Bin Ramke, Broc Rossell, Eleni Sikelianos, Sampson Starkweather, Mathias Svalina, Paige Taggart, G.C. Waldrep, Jared White, Megan Whitman, Elizabeth Willis, Benh Zeitlin. Particular thanks to my family, and also the students and faculty in the Literature and Creative Writing PhD program at the University of Denver.

"Fill Me with Poison!" is for Bill Cassidy.

"Practice by Fire & Doubt" is for Bin Ramke.

JULIA COHEN's first full-length book, *Triggermoon Triggermoon*, was published in 2011, and her third collection, *I Was Not Born*, will be released by Noemi Press in 2014. Her poems and lyric essays appears in such journals as *jubilat*, *New American Writing*, *Kenyon Review Online*, *Colorado Review*, *DIAGRAM*, and *Black Warrior Review*.

IT MOVES IN, IS NOT STATIC

Abdomen   domain

Where I store my arrows